# Miracle Temple

# THE DREAMSEEKER POETRY SERIES

Books in the DreamSeeker Poetry Series, intended to make available fine writing by Anabaptist-related poets, are published by Cascadia Publishing House under the DreamSeeker Books imprint and often copublished with Herald Press. Cascadia oversees content of these poetry collections in collaboration with the DreamSeeker Poetry Series Editor Jeff Gundy (Jean Janzen volumes 1-4) as well as in consultation with its Editorial Council and the authors themselves.

1. On the Cross
   *By Dallas Wiebe, 2005*
2. I Saw God Dancing
   *By Cheryl Denise Miller, 2005*
3. Evening Chore
   *By Shari Wagner, 2005*
4. Where We Start
   *By Debra Gingerich, 2007*
5. The Coat Is Thin
   *By Leonard Neufeldt, 2008*
6. Miracle Temple
   *By Esther Stenson, 2009*
7. Storage Issues
   *By Suzanne Miller, 2010*
8. Face to Face: A Poetry Collection
   *By Julie Cadwallader-Staub, 2010*

Also worth noting are two poetry collections that would likely have been included in the series had it been in existence then:

1. Empty Room with Light
   *By Ann Hostetler, 2002*
2. A Liturgy for Stones
   *By David Wright, 2003*

# Miracle Temple

Poems by
**Esther Yoder Stenson**

**DreamSeeker Poetry Series, Volume 6**

**DreamSeeker Books**
TELFORD, PENNSYLVANIA

*an imprint of*
Cascadia Publishing House LLC

*Copublished with*
Herald Press
Scottdale, Pennsylvania

**Cascadia Publishing House orders, information, reprint permissions:**
contact@CascadiaPublishingHouse.com
1-215-723-9125
126 Klingerman Road, Telford PA 18969
www.CascadiaPublishingHouse.com

*Miracle Temple*
Copyright © 2009 by Cascadia Publishing House, Telford, PA 18969
All rights reserved
DreamSeeker Books is an imprint of Cascadia Publishing House LLC
Copublished with Herald Press, Scottdale, PA
Library of Congress Catalog Number: 2009036768
**ISBN 13:** 978-1-931038-68-3; **ISBN 10:** 1-931038-68-6
Book design by Cascadia Publishing House
Cover design by Gwen M. Stamm
Cover photo: Aunt Amelia at Brook Lane Farm.
As she writes in her diary of that time on June 22, 1949, "Pulled weeds in flowerbeds. Ada snapped my picture while I was down on my honkers pulling weeds."

The paper used in this publication is recycled and meets the
minimum requirements of American National Standard for Information
Sciences—Permanence of Paper for Printed Library Materials, ANSI Z39.48-1984.1984

"Lessons," "Backache Saga," and "False Teeth" were first published in *Dreamseeker Magaazine*, and "Snake Stories" in the blog *The New Verse News*, newversenews.blogspot.com.

**Library of Congress Cataloguing-in-Publication Data**
Stenson, Esther Yoder, 1951-
Miracle temple : poems / by Esther Yoder Stenson.
  p. cm. -- (Dreamseeker poetry series ; v. 6)
  Summary: "Here are poems expressing two different voices--one that of Aunt Amelia as channeled by her niece Esther Stenson, the other that of Stenson herself." "[summary]"--Provided by publisher.
  ISBN-13: 978-1-931038-68-3 (5.5 x 8.5" trade pbk. : alk. paper)
  ISBN-10: 1-931038-68-6 (5.5 x 8.5" trade pbk. : alk. paper)
  I. Title.
  PS3619.T4764776M57 2009
  811'.6--dc22
                    2009036768

17 16 15 14 13 12 11 10 09    10 9 8 7 6 5 4 3 2 1

*To Aunt Amelia, my* Glook

# Contents

## I
The Fire • 15
Shadow and Light • 17
Girlie Civets • 19
Bees (1939) • 21
Backache Saga • 22
False Teeth • 25
Lessons • 27
Soul Mate • 29
Desperation • 31
Seed • 33
My Beeplin' • 35
The Bishop • 38

## II
Brook Lane Farm • 41
Conversion • 43
Pineville, Kentucky • 46
Tampa • 48
A Woman's Power • 51
Tending Fowl • 52
Affirmation • 54

## III
Santa Ana Rock'n Roll • 49
Electronics Factory • 60
L. A. Maid • 62
God's Child • 65
Miracle Temple • 67
For the Joy • 69
You'd a Been Proud • 70
Aunt Melia's Lament • 72

## IV
Aunt Amelia's Alchemy • 77
Grandpa • 79
Sunday Sermons • 81
Light in the Hay Mow • 82
Shadows • 85

## V
Innocent abroad • 89
They • 92
Veracruz, Mexico • 94
Babel • 97
Soulmate II • 99
For I Was a Stranger • 101
Interlude • 102
Lijiang, China • 103

## VI
Rooted in Earth • 107
Clean Air Act • 110
Holy Ire • 111
Water • 113
Snake Stories • 115
Temples • 117
Tom's Garden • 118
Life Cycles • 119

*The Author*   *120*

I

*From Amelia, with love.*

## *The Fire*

Neighbors runnin' across dry fields, shoutin' and wavin'
finally made us understand the smoke I smelled in the
        basement
was connected to flames already burstin' out of attic
        windows
like a picture I'd only seen in a storybook.

My brothers' guns and shells, ready for huntin',
exploded in upstairs heat like we was havin' war.

Our kitchen stove was fulla berry pies half-baked that
rolled out like giant coins from a shaken piggy bank
when the oven door jiggled open as strong arms carried
it out to the yard, a big pot o' fried chicken—all we had
left for dinner—simmerin' on its top for hungry men
workin' on our new poultry house.

Mom went frantic cryin' for John and Alvin,
laid sleepin' upstairs, till she knew someone carried them,
mattress and all, away to the apple orchard on the hill.
Then she yanked odd clothes off hooks,
and stuffed them in our spare oven in the yard,
the only clothes that survived.

The Allensville fire truck had trouble pushin' through
all the good Samaritans fillin' our lane, and when it did,
couldn't find water fast enough to save a thing.
Brother Jake was too shocked to pour even the
one dishpan full he held in his hand.

All our toys—treasures made or got from the sink hole—
went up in smoke, while the big orange-brown china press
fulla glass bowls and plates was carried sideways
from the livin' room with not a dish broke.

Our basement fulla summer's canning was left
with fruit jars boiled to half while we never
got a chance to taste seven gallons of
newly boiled apple butter stored in the attic.
The whole community, Amish or not,
gave us so much food and clothes to
make it through the winter
some black soul warned that
if God was punishin' us we wouldn't feel it.

And I, nicknamed "Fuss,"
was struck dumb for once
just staring
as brother Lee kicked the last wooden fragments
into the smoldering ashes of my childhood.

## Shadow and Light

Don't DO that to me!
I yelled
over and over.

"No matter how loud you holler
no one's gonna hear you"
he taunted that evening,
everyone else gone visiting,
us two left alone to
milk cows in the barn.

After Stover Jake did that to me
I cried so much his parents,
who kept me after our house
burned on the lower farm,
took me back to my
parents on the upper farm,
mistaking a small girl's sore body
and spirit for mere loneliness.

Mother's "we don't have no place now"
added salt to injury oozing pain
that could not find words in
my terrified seven-year-old self
violated beyond my soiled
evidence tossed over the fence.

When big cigar-smoking Josh Peachy asked
if he could take me to their house, I didn't
know what to think, or what new torture
was in store. But kind as God,
with a penny a day he bought me
lollipops like rainbow colored suns
chasing away my heart's shadows.

And every night fifteen-year-old Rudy
made me a frothy chocolate
shake from creamy milk extracted
fresh by hand that day to keep me from
minding the absence of my house
full of brothers, giving me back a little
bit of faith in what is called man.

## Girlie Civets

With a name like Alforetta,
I don't know why people called her Girlie Civets.
Looked more like a ghost than a girlie to me
with her thin body, a face I never remembered,
and a house fulla what I didn't care to see.

People said her bedroom was so fulla rats
she slept sittin' up in her kitchen rocker
which was why I always ran like a banty
past her gray lookin' unpainted place, afraid
a rat or horde of mice would come at me
—or else I took the long way 'round to
Water Street to see Seth's Mary rather than
risk being bitten by ugly sharp little teeth.

Alone in the world, didn't have family.
Big Valley's well fed needed someone
to receive their charity, so they fetched
her bags of groceries and homemade stuff.

My mom sometimes made me take her
a loaf fresh from the bakehouse,
or a hunka newly butchered pork I poked
into her waiting hands through the door
cracked barely wide enough for me
to remember what the insides looked like,
hardly daring even a peek before
dashing back home to safety.

Rockin' at night, rockin' on her feet
days, she sloshed my grandmother's
buttermilk right outta the jar full
she gave her one day.

But she never complained.
Took what was offered but never asked,
and sometimes refused—like the time
someone offered to take her apron,
her topmost layer, home to wash
to be more fittin' for company.
"Oh no," she said, "took it off once
last winter and caught a cold."

Perhaps under all those clothes,
all those layers of stockings pulled off
on her last trip to the hospital was
an angel I never knew because
my own layers kept me from
seein' the real Girlie Civets
—whose name sang Alforetta.

## Bees  (1939)

Oh the bees, the bees, the bees!
Swarmed around the honey I served
at Hettie's table, makin' me near crazy
for fear they'd buzz up under my skirt
lookin' for more honey.

Oh, the people, the people!
Just like the bees, seven thousand souls
 flocked to the tent that looked like
a giant bee-hive on twelve acres of land
my Dad loaned to the General Conference
since the Mennonites were so good to us
after our fire it woulda been sin to refuse,
even if the Amish bishop did tell
all his members to stay away.

Mom loved all that singin', strollin' slowly past,
pretendin' to visit the neighbors while drinkin' in
"I Will be True to Thee," worryin' about brother Lee
lest he marry some Mennonite powder puff or butterfly,
yet believin' somethin' good must come from
the gath'rin' of so many from twenty-three states,
marv'lin' at how automobiles came so far, so fast
how some people flew in, circlin' overhead,
like the bees, before landin' in the field,
lookin' for honey.

## *Backache Saga*

The day Aunt Katie let my
tiny body fall back from
her arms with a jerk,
like a rag doll,
I cried all day like a knife
had done cut me through
for good.

Pain followed my years like
that dog Mickey followed
us everywhere.

Still my brothers made me
drive the horse attached to
the hay wagon over rutted
fields, cultivate corn and
arrange shocks in endless rows.
My back felt like plowed earth.
Sleep was impossible.

The brace around my torso for
three hot summers, beginning
with my sixteenth year, was so
unbearable I took a yardstick
to scratch the driving-me-crazy itch
inside the metal cast.
It didn't do a bit a good.

Finally, Dr. Cassidy said I'd be
paralyzed if I refused last-chance
surgery in Lewistown.

They cut me open like a carcass,
used silver bolts and burrs to
fasten femur from my leg onto
backbone while 'bout every doctor on
the East Coast, like a circle of
curious cows, stood around my bed
observing this experimental operation.

I never saw Dad cryin' like he did
when we thought I was dyin' after
my second awful feverish day.
He had to leave me with Mother
to await the clock's eleventh hour
and I believe he must've been
pray'in hard as my fate approached.
The moment came and
I felt a change comin' over me
sure as I'm sittin' here.
Under no medication
the pain and fever slunk
away like a whipped cur,
and life coursed through my
body like when God first
breathed into Adam.

That night I slept so good
I was sittin' up eatin' the first
breakfast I'd wanted in days
when my Dad walked in
off the milk truck he'd hitched
a ride on, looked at me like he was
seein' the Resurrection, and repeated
"I can't believe it! I can't believe it!"

## *False Teeth (1939)*

Eighteen years old,
my teeth all rotten like
kernels gone bad
when Mom took me
to Lewistown to pull 'em
all for twenty dollars—
no fillin' teeth
those days.

Ran away from callers and
covered my ugly flat mouth
nine months of Sundays with
flowerdy hankies to keep
folks from seein' how
my nose and mouth met like
an ol' hag as gums
shrank to proper size for
new forty-five-dollar chompers.

Fittin' day I preened like a
peacock, goin' home,
till I stopped at McCrory's
to buy straight pins for Mom.
My mouth suddenly felt fulla nails.
The dime store clerk seein' my
big black bonnet, pointin' finger
and garbled Jr-rr-rr, must've thought
I was some dumb Dutchman
that couldn't speak proper English.

But it was better'n havin'
a mouth fulla lies
like some o' those ol' men
up in Washington
nowadays.

## Lessons

"And what do people do when
they have a date?" I asked one
who was older and wiser in
the ways of *rum springa*.

"You lie down like this,
put your arms around him
like so," she instructed.

"Just like the pigs!" I snorted,
amazed that human activities
find their parallel on our family farm.

So when a visiting "Pequaer"
asked me for a date, I was ready.
After the singin' at John Byler's
we two, joined by my brother
and his companion, bundled in their
big bed upstairs—four across—
like cigars lyin' in a box
waitin' for a light.

Took but a few moments for the
animal beside me to commence,
shiftin' himself to the position
that freed my foot to
let go a mighty kick,
pitchin' him onto the floor
into the cold.

"Let's go home!" I hissed to my brother.

So without a word, he left his
gal of brief acquaintance and
marched with me up the long lane
through the seething night.

## *Soul Mate*

Even though he took Sadie home
after the taffy pulling and never
offered explanation or reason why
he chose not to see me again after
more than a year of laughter
and intimate conversations.

Even though I walked five miles
one Saturday eve with Lizzie,
disguised in my brother's clothes,
to take apart his buggy in
trite revenge for tramplin' my heart—
only to have him catch me in the act
and grab my foot as I was
hoppin' across the wire fence,
causin' me to lose balance and
fall on the hard ground,
breakin' my arm severely.

Even though I had to run
those five miles back home
clutchin' my achin' arm
to my achin' heart.

Even though on Sunday I had to
hide the arm in long sleeves,
pinning cape to dress with one hand
before jolting in a horse-drawn buggy to
the house where Amish church required
sittin' for hours on hard backless bench.

Even though on Monday Dr. Miller jerked
the broken bones back in place and I
was privileged to stay with Grandma Peachey,
only to face her anger at next Sunday's
discovery that I'd slipped out
to the Mennonite church with Dorothy,
and had to go home again before I was ready.

Even though I left Pennsylvania for Virginia,
Florida, Kentucky, Ohio, California,
and Virginia again.

Even though I am eighty-three,
I still feel
he was my soul mate.

## *Desperation*

Mattie was in Iowa with her sweetheart
and Naomi with hers in Hagerstown,
leavin' me, a young bloom in 1942,
the only woman in the house to care for Mom
lyin' so delirious with smallpox that she knocked
the medicine right out of grandpa's hand,
laughin' into his angry swearin' face,
her usual gentle submission
gone the way of the wind.

When the pox pushed right through
the bunions on her bony little feet
no one knew what to do.
There was no escape from my older brother's
insistence that I go out and milk the cows,
clean the house, churn enough butter
and crank enough icecream to feed the whole neighbor-
      hood.
The milk trucks could not enter Big Valley
after guests comin' by train from Ohio
to Ezra's wedding brought the deadly virus.
Nobody could leave. Having escaped
on his honeymoon to Lancaster,
my brother could not come back with his bride.

Finally I couldn't take anymore.
I waited one night till all were in bed and
flew down the snowy lane like a chicken uncooped
to Levi Eshes place to call Naomi—tell her
she HAD to come home before me or Mom died
I wasn't sure which.
The train conductor didn't want to leave her off
in that cursed place, but Naomi, who never took "No"
marched right home and rescued me
until Mom rallied and found her
submission once again.

## Seed

White chickenfeed sacks flapping on long wash line—
like flags proclaiming allegiance to no place but ours—
served for more than the usual underwear
and dishcloths the day my sister Naomi
miscarried her firstborn with so much blood
I thought she'd drown in it before we
yanked the bags off the line to stanch
the flow and clean her up,
the whiteness turning dark crimson
like wool on a sacrificed lamb.

I filled up the zuvver* to bathe
the barely formed boy no longern' my hand,
which, still damp from its washing,
slipped suddenly from my palm
directly into a cigar box fulla beet seed
accident'ly bumped from its shelf over the
brick oven in the bake house, cov'ring
the spotless body with dark specks
like shaken pepper misplaced;
our mouths jerked O!

Mom was afraid if we buried it in the garden,
seed would sprout in the shape of a little human,
a living reminder of that awful day,
so I wrapped the babe in clean white cloth,
reverently arranged it in the emptied box,
and with faces bowed, laid it to rest
in the hole we women dug under the grapevine
where spring spadings would not disturb.

I couldn't believe how seeds grew one by one,
year after year in my sister's womb,
filling her home with eight
whose seeds are now
scattered all over.

*wash-tub

## My "Beeplin"

Never wanted a baby hangin' out over my belly,
puttin' a strain on my weak back, or stayin'
in bed nine days like they used to then.

Never minded not havin' my own, as
my brothers and sisters spilled their quivers
over into my arms, glad for a *glook* to *gnotch* them.

Joe's Bennie, the first, was spoiled rotten smart, but
I never stayed there late enough to chance bein'
picnic for the bears, as I outran the sun home.

Kore's Alvin was a good kid, steady as our Nell.
The sun hid its face the day his tractor
upended on the hill and pinned him under.

Jake's Esther was my dollbaby with
her midnight hair on a teeny head
not much bigger'n a teacup.

For Mattie's Paul I traveled to Iowa.
Never thought he'd repay me for goin' that far by
aimin' his teetee, like an arc, right into my mouth.

Alvin's first five—now that's a story.
When gentle Sharon was born I bought me a jersey
heifer that was honey-colored like a wild doe.
Because I loved my beeplin I promised Alvin its
first born to give milk for his first born, but instead
the dumb cow died and I coulda cried.

Wasn't long before Annie swelled again like
a giant seed after rain, so we couldn't say
we was shocked seein' double when the seed ripened.
Paul's loud WAH left no mistake he was a little man
but Pauline—I declare I'd never heard a baby
I liked to hear cry the way she sang—sweet as
the life she lived and left too soon, her pain
spidered out, wrapping us all up in it.

Next trip to the hospital, I sat with Alvin
nervous as a young bull and dancin' around
till the nurse told him to come and have a look.
His jaws dropped all the way to the floor;
his eyes exploded.
Never thought Annie's little womb could
carry two again—but what did we know?

Now that was a job!

I was tryin' to feed the babies that had sucked up
all their mother's sap and runnin' back'n forth
to check on Annie—babies cryin' I told
Alvin, never used to hangin' clothes and cookin'
"you gotta help me" and I reckon he learned
'bout as much then as he learned goin' to college.

Never got paid a red dime for washin' hundreds of
smelly diapers, countless meals made, cows milked,
miles went and spent for my brothers and sisters

But all those babies were my *beeplin*
*Ich gleich dich. Weist du sell?!\**


*beeplin*—little chicks
*glook*—old cluck
*gnotch*—to spoil or take care of lovingly

*I love you. Do you know that?

### The Bishop

If my mother's brother-in-law didn't want to
rule all Amish churches like my mom said,
he sure liked tellin' my dad how to raise us kids,
creakin' in the lane with his black buggy while I
sneaked around back of our house to listen.

Breathin' down our necks, he made brother Jonas
go back to the seamstress to have another *mutza* made
before he blessed the union with Mollie.

Kicked brother Joe outta church for a year's
worth of sowin' wild oats, comin' home
short-haired from the wild west.

Put out Dave for marryin' his lovin' sweet-cookin'
round-faced Nancy from the Byler church
outta line with his straight and narrow.

Put off my sister Mattie marryin' her sweetheart
seven plus years before admitting Sam was no unbeliever,
finally givin' permission to tie their knot in faraway Iowa.

Lookin' down his knobby nose,
the more he laid down the law to my dad
the more I wanted to find grace.

The day I heard Dad tell him to go home,
look after his own, sayin' he'd do his
best with his, it was all I could do to
hold back a big snort!

# II

## *Brook Lane Farm (1949)*

I liked workin' in the kitchen best.
Here was order.
Knives and forks knew their places,
dishwater did its duty,
plates calmly waited and
food did not threaten or scream.

Otherwise,
I thought I would go nuts like the rest
when I had to sit tight by the beds
of the shock exhausted.
The moment they came to
I had to be calm—tell 'em
it's gonna be okay.

One day bedside, I suddenly
found a stark staring eye fix on me
like a spell when my sudden move
made her let out a high screech and
startled me so terrific I hollered back.
The passing hall attendant said
between our alternating shrieks
he didn't know which was which.

Another day, I took a man out to the garden
to take in fresh air bird songs
to calm his nerves—prob'ly mine too.
Pullin' piles of weeds and pickin' up
stones to smooth ground for plantin'
I kept on the thin lid of my composure
till the guy took it right off sayin'
"bet ya thought I was goin' ta throw
one at ya." My heart goin' pit-a-pat
pit-a-pat, I lied "of course not!"

I guess I wasn't ready for an
unsteady world outside the kitchen
where I couldn't win the battle
with my jitters which is
what ya gotta do if you're
gonna help anybody
in a place like that
—or anyplace.

## *Conversion 1952*

Half-way down the long lane on the old home place
the sink hole gaped like the mouth of sin I was
seekin' to flee that evening when my Amish
12-year-old self sneaked out of the house through
tall corn rows to listen to the Mennonite evangelist
at the Allensville church near the end of our lane.
In spite of Dorothy Hartzler's insistence that I
go in, I stayed hunched outside in the bushes—
fearful of my Dad's anger—but more terrified
of the wrath that was to come if I did not
somehow find my peace with God.

Seein' that I wasn't satisfied with things as they were,
my sister said, "I'm afraid you'll go English"—
cease to be Amish, become an outsider.
But that wasn't what I was after.

I did not know how or when I could handily
escape this place and my burden of sin,
but I told God if He ever made a hole for me,
I would slip through it and fly far,
far away from the tradition and ignorance
that finally even my father could not tolerate
when the Amish bishop required him to
shun his son, David. Couldn't eat at our table.
"Before I do that to my own son," he said,
"I'll move away! He never did anything wrong
at home. I can't do that!" So in 1943, he took
what was left of our family to Virginia.

The hole I longed for opened a tiny slit
as I found myself in a place where
the Word could be read freely, and my
desire for God grew like the unfolding vine of
a morning glory curling toward the sun.
Only, the pole was too short and my growing
faith could not find all it searched for
in the sheltered community
of Amish Mennonites.

One night's vision in the long black shed,
of a whole bunch of little angels whooshin'
down to carry me home, left me tremblin'
with fear of everlastin' judgment and I knew
I still HAD to do somethin'.
So with Mom and Dad, and my friend, Katie,
I went to Florida for the winter.
Spring sent them home, but Katie and I
extended into summer.

Finally durin' Sarasota revivals I felt ready
to commit myself to God. I walked boldly
down the grassy path to the wooden altar
under George Brunk's enormous tent
to claim my peace as he loudly preached
"The Whole Gospel for the Whole World"
to huge crowds. I felt SO GOOD.
That was when I was REALLY converted.

My dad and Ben Troyer did not
think there was any more "gospel" we
needed, so down from Virginia they
came to confront the Mennonite
evangelist who they were sure had
brainwashed their daughters, stolen
them away from their Amish faith.

They marched right up to him
demanding an explanation.
Brunk tried to get them converted
sayin', "let's get down on our knees—
let's pray about it!" While Troyer
mumbled refusal, my dad, not bein'
used to prayin' without "the book"
finally managed a brief, but fitting
 "God be merciful to me, a sinner."
And Brunk, in our defense, stated,
"It's up to them, it's their decision,
I didn't force them; no one did."

So our dads went back.
We didn't.

### *Pineville, Kentucky 1954*

First time away from my
weed-free shoo-fly pie world,
where money was scarce as
coon's eggs, but people the happiest
I ever saw—instead of cash
in the offering, gave what they had
of meat, potatoes, carrots,
beans, and onions—yes, onions
enough to feed the five thousand
but it was only me'n Katie,
Reverend Jackson, his wife'n kid
to fry up the whole bushel we
made into onion rings, browned
with potatoes and everything else
in the gallons of Crisco given us.

Jackson preached so hard,
he preached the mountain folk
right out of the summer woods,
walkin' for miles, lanterns swingin'
among dusky shadows never touched
by light other than the occasional moon
—dry souls so hungry for God
they did not mind sittin' for hours
every night for two months on
splintery planks laid across rough hewn
chunks of wood around a sleepin'
pot-bellied stove in a
ramshackledy old church.

When they weren't porch sittin'
or goin' to meetin', they were
grubbin' in the hills so steep
people said potatoes scraped
from shallow earth
rolled right smack down
into the mouth of gaping
gunny sacks, like marbles
down a marble roller.

Jackson's mother-in-law
loaned us her creaky old house
where bedbugs bit like crazy
forcing us after first night
to drag our mattress outside
to let the sun scorch the critters
into bug hell—after which we set
each bed leg carefully in cans
of kerosene. Sprayed so much,
we almost killed ourselves,
but for all the funny stuff we
heard and saw that summer
—Katie and I—
we more nearly died laughin'.
.

## *Tampa*

"Didn't know beans from dogs"—
one suitcase—all the clothes I had
as I stepped off the Greyhound and
walked up Tampa Avenue to find myself
or someplace or somebody.

I had to get a hold of myself,
cryin' so many bushels of tears
Brother Jackson didn't know
if I was fit to hit the gospel trail
—I had to make up my mind.

Three blocks later Revival Temple
appeared with doors wide open like
heaven's gate, invitin' me to enter
—get down on my knees
alongside everyone else
pourin' out their hearts, seekin' God.

The black woman attached to the arm
extended around my shoulder said God
plainly told her to invite me home.
"You in trouble?" she asked
"Not in trouble—just want direction—
like Jesus when he left the
ordinary places to wander in the
desert so He could hear God's voice."

I found she spoke the truth when
she said "You're in the right place."
Noon prayers every day
and soulful sermons every night
just lifted my spirit so terrific
—above the fears of
what they would say,
what they would think,
those whom I loved
but misunderstood me.

Like God in person she was,
heatin' bricks for my cold bed,
listenin' to my muddled pain,
tellin' me how, like the raven fed Elisha,
food appeared when she laid
her list on the sideboard with no
time for grocery shoppin' sayin'
God I need this and I need that.

Even angels shouldn't be abused,
so I moved near the church,
roomed over a restaurant where
I got up before daylight to serve coffee
to burly cigar factory workers
from across the street
and run the cash register
til news came of Dave's death.

That angel gave me train fare for Lewistown;
I left with just the clothes on my back
and because I never returned, I still
don't know what happened to the furniture
and silverware I stored in her attic
—which didn't matter because
I had all I needed to move on.

## A Woman's Power

Thought for sure my family would
all shake their heads, frowning
when I stepped off the train in
Lewistown for brother Dave's funeral
without that little white cap
upstanding Amish and Mennonite
women wear on their head to
give them some kind of power
—they have more than you think.

But no one said a thing
—just so glad to see me—except
my sister Naomi, who wasn't afraid
to tell any of us what to do, insisted
I put on at least a little black scarf among
the dark dresses and long faces of the funeral
crowd gathered in the barn, afraid of
whispering stares and family honor lost if
I didn't have somethin' on my head.

I said what's the difference
I don't usually wear nothin' anyway,
but to make her hush I wore what
she called my *"spott dichli,"
never thinkin' she would one day
leave the Amish and wear
one exactly like it!

*mock cloth

### Tending Fowl

Never thought I'd look at another fowl
after tendin' thirty coops, each holdin'
one hundred turkey chicks for
Weavers Hatchery in Stuarts Draft.
Amanda and I lived upstairs in the
lower house on Norman Yoder's farm
right next to our "babies."

We strained our backs carryin' water
twice a day like Chinese coolies,
kept fire in coal stoves to warm the little peeps,
and worked ourselves silly after Weaver
sold to Ed Mast who did nothing but
drive circles around the farm,
perched on the seat of his buggy
like a banty rooster to make sure
we had no moment of rest.

But after givin' my car to Brother Jackson, and
comin' back to Virginia to work after Dave's funeral,
I had no choice.

While I walked the half mile to
the poultry plant around the sharp bend
on Tinkling Spring Road and
stood all day starin' at the hind ends of
pimpled plucked chickens hung
by their necks on rotating chains,
reached into those hind ends as fast as I could
and pulled out stinkin' guts,
leavin' my hands hot and wrinkled
as dried peach skin at day's end.

While I fed and watered five hundred
baby turkeys in a coop up on the hill
in the apple orchard on Dad's farm,
and slept on top of the coop at night
with my brothers and a gun to scare off
foxes lookin' for turkey dumplin's,

Jackson was drivin' my car
from Florida all the way to Oregon

While I paid for it.

## Affirmation

Lizzie sold me Davie's car for three
hundred fifty since she didn't want
people talkin', it sittin' on her Amish
farm while her lyin' son was in jail.

Old Buick so ugly inside I covered the
floor with carpet so I could stand four
thousand miles lookin' at it,
leavin' home again for another
episode of my forty years exile
in the wilderness followin' the trav'lin'
evangelist I'd last seen in Florida.

Jackson met me in West Virginia and I
puttered after him all the way to the Golden Gate—
no idea what I was gettin' into.

No money kept us drivin' day and night,
God watchin' over the time we came upon
a shacky old roadside cabin with two beds,
plopped down sleep-starved in our clothes
and prayed no one and no thing would
come in and get us while we zonked out.

Though I'd already cried bushels,
not wantin' to hurt my mom
by leavin' her, leavin' the Amish way,
I knew I was followin' God's servant
when he placed his white hanky over
the finger I smashed in the car door one day
and prayin' earnestly, stopped the bleedin' pain
before my very eyes.

III

## Santa Ana Rock & Roll

So this country girl could stand
livin' by the Santa Ana freeway
I got in mind I was listenin' to the
shwe shwe of the Pacific Ocean when
one morning after I was dressed for work
the bedroom door slammed on my back
spooky like, I said "What is this?!"

The foundations of my place trembled
as if it had a bad case of Parkinson's;
I saw little Mikey's cage swingin'
scatterin' feathers in the livin' room and
realized the earth was on the move.

Only some Divine finger must've
fastened my feet inside one more minute
while chimney bricks tumbled like
poked dominoes onto the path I always
took around the corner of the house,
leavin' nothin' but tar paper hangin' loose
like my quakin' heart.

### *Electronics Factory (L.A. 1966-1975)*

They didn't care how much I slaved
for forty cents an hour when I was able
then threw me out after nine years of
standin' on my feet peerin' through glass
to protect my eyes, wearin' plastic gloves,
plastic sleeves, plastic aprons.
I became a plastic robot cleansing
nuts and bolts meticulously lest
one tiny drop of acid on my skin
would go straight to my blood
and poison me to the bone
like the acid
in the raindrops
in the runoff
in the rivers
in the groundwaters
poisoning our mother earth.

Now is not the acid eating into the brains,
into the hearts of honchos everywhere?
So when our health is broken
we are flicked off lightly as a
swatted fly, a speck o' soot or
poured down the drain
like the water
like the acid
like the alcohol
I rinsed them in before laying them
flat on pans to purify under infrared
so the bowels of modern gadgets
would move smoothly no matter
that with each passing year we
move less and wear out more.

## L.A Maid

Will they remember how hard we worked
to keep the façade of Beverly Hills clean
white, down to the light uniforms we had
to wear so if anybody came to those
mansion doors we'd not disgrace them?

Used to make me so mad—
having to iron all these uniforms
but at least they let me go through their
bags of clothes before the Salvation Army
got their share, and pick out things I needed.
Nothin' fancy—except I used to like
spiffy hats sporting a feather from some
bird that never intended his clothes be
used to decorate human finery.

One classy place I worked had an
upstairs maid and a downstairs maid.
I was the downstairs maid.
Didn't like the upstairs—too many
beds to fix and bathrooms to clean for
every one of those eight huge bedrooms
—three or four beds in some.
Didn't know why so few people needed so
many bathrooms—if they had a whole
bunch of people living there
nights after parties or what.

For one night's party I babysat
little Cristy in an upstairs bedroom far
from the noisy bunch when who comes
in the door but Mr. Cowboy himself—
the one I was watchin' on TV! A gentleman
and good-lookin'. Asked if I'd mind if he
watched his show with us. Boy did I ever not!
I'd jump up and down and spit purple beans
if I could remember his name.
—Oh, would you believe
I think it was Clint Eastwood!

A good thing about their outlandish parties
—the women would set leftover meat on the worktable
leavin' a note sayin' we could take what we
wanted before it got thrown away—
sometimes I'd get half a leg o' lamb or
a big ol' pile o' ham. Took a shoppin' bag
along sometimes in case I'd get somethin'
to take home. Like the woman said to Jesus,
"Even the dogs get the crumbs from the master's table."

But one thing I said I'd never do.
The community women waited to shop
till just the time we maids went home.
These women were sittin' on those bus seats
with all their baggage spread around them
and when we maids got on—tireder than
I don't know what—we had to stand for
miles and miles just holdin' to the bars
with our bags. That used to grit on me—
I'd've been embarrassed to act like that.

Little Lindsey—one child I looked after—would
ask me at night to please kill the mockinbird
singin' constantly keepin' her awake.
I said no.
I ain't killin' what God made.

## God's Child

He was at the end of the row
when IQ's were handed out,
didn't go to school with
other children his age before
all the rules were made
mixin' 'em all together;
he was so kind
never complained or
whined like some
born into more money
than an entire African country.

We two walked one day
down a Pasadena mountainside
to gather scarlet petals
dropped from Rose Bowl
floats, and coming back tired
paused by a bench where
the boy laid his head on
my lap resting
before returning to his
beloved room full of
electric train where I
sat with him hours while
his mother lay so sick
in bed I thought she had
some terrible disease, and
was shocked by the
discovery she was
pregnant with his
little sister.

Why didn't I stay forever,
lovin' that child,
fresh as cedar after rain
and sweet as purple clover?

## Miracle Temple

Worked myself bone tired every day
cleaning mansions for movie stars
to pay the mortgage on Miracle Temple
where all kinds of people,
brown, white, Spanish, Japanese, Chinese
— you name it, they had 'em all –
sang and clapped as I pulled apart a
hundred and twenty bass
accordion so heavy I needed
a chair to prop me up,
justa playin', havin' me a good time,
astonishin' even myself with
the harmony that came outta
those ivory keys and buttons;
honest to goodness I didn't
know a note from a note;
as the Spirit led, so we played—
Mrs. J and I—
every night but Mondays.

While all that mixed up congregation and
music makin' was enough miracle,
I couldn't believe that
all the grass I cut with a push mower,
all the diapers changed on stinky babes,
weeds I yanked with calloused hands, and
all the meals I prepared for the
Jacksons wasn't enough to turn into
even a tiny drop of Cana's wine
my weekly payment from Reverend J
—one can of pineapple juice!

## *For the Joy*

Had I not felt the hand of Someone
on my shoulder when I asked God
where He was, not sure if I was
doin' the right thing,

had I not seen Jackson was for the people
not himself, when instead of chasin' mammon
he chose forsaken old churches and preached
to crowds too poor to give a dollar,

had I not experienced God anointing
my tongue with words I didn't make up myself,
witnessed the feverish and injured healed with
no ointment but fasting and prayer,

had I not seen Watts burning, goin' crazy
yet had courage to continue worshipping
in that stealin' killin' angry neighborhood
our temple spared, our congregation growin',

I could not have worked so hard
slept so little
given so much
and been so happy.

### *You'd a Been Proud*

You woulda been proud, Mr. King
when my dad, back in the 1940's
asked Ed Brown, who cleaned our chicken house,
to share our meat and potatoes
despite his nervous protests
"I can't be seen here, I can't be seen here!"

You woulda been proud when my dad answered
"Don't worry, I'll take care of that" and
wouldn't allow this warm-hearted black man
to go home without sharing our lunch in the days
when most of Virginia still put
The Great Wall between black and white.

You'd a been proud of my mom for urging
Mrs. Edna Washington, born of a slave,
to come in anytime for coffee, when the
old lady, half scared of us whites, walked
up the long, dusty, rutted lane by the back fields
to fetch her drinking water at our spring.

My mom and dad who came from the north,
had no use for the way their southern neighbors
looked down their long white noses
and put signs on their public places to
separate one human being from another.

And you mighta been proud of me
when later I left those proper, well-meaning
but stiff-collared Sarasota Mennonites
and paid no heed to those who asked if
I wasn't scared goin' to New Town church
with all those black people to hear Rev'rend Jackson,
to go where my spirit felt its burning.

You mighta raised an eyebrow at my
followin' this Jackson all over the U.S.,
helpin' in his mission to save the lost,
forgettin' about layin' up treasure for my old age
But you'd a been proud I never let
no one's skin color keep me
from goin' anywhere
from prayin' with anyone
from livin' in any neighborhood
doin' what I believed was Jesus' way
—just like Mom and Dad showed me.

(For MLK, January 17, 2005)

### Aunt Melia's Lament

It's not goin' that good anymore.

Us children used to walk anywhere:
down the long lane, up cool berried woods,
across nubby fields, into Allensville;
We never feared nobody.

Now you don't know who you're dancin' with
who you're lookin' at, what they're thinkin' of
where they might dump you.

They don't know how to be decent anymore.

At home us fourteen had to shut our mouths up and
kiss the one we fussed with, the only way we survived.
We had discipline.

Now those big mouths on TV talk so ugly you
can't trust them any more than a tornado;
makes me so mad I turn the dumb thing off.

They can't do without anything anymore.
Now they have to have every beeping, blinking, burping,
push-button, wind-up, ding-y new thing on
the market—grownups and kids alike.

We played with mud—
made mud pies, mud forts, mud roads
mud figures, mud anything and everything.

Maybe it's time everyone got down
and PLAYED in the mud again
instead of THROWIN' it all the time.

It's not goin' that good anymore.

# IV

## Aunt Amelia's Alchemy (to Amelia)

In the way your beaming frankness expressed itself
I found definitions not held by most people
in my frugal Amish community.

Jezebel's scarlet became the color on God's palette
most favored to decorate flora and fauna
simply to dazzle and delight the eyes.

"Worldly" 78's spinning out second-hand music
in English taught my small attentive ears
their first gospel choruses.

In your hands, cast-off seashells from Pinecraft Beach
became kittens, birds, and bunnies for a Christmas
basement full of us wide-eyed wonderlings.

The sour fruits of citrus became sunsweet delicacies
piled high with brown kissed meringue
served to Governor Knight and the rest of us alike.

The emptiness of your absence became a sequence
of long letters from Easter Street or Sunset Boulevard
coloring the window overlooking the hedge of my youth.

The drudgery of your hard-earned wages became joy
when you gave your car to an Oregon family stranded,
or sent us savored mounds of See's Candy in the mail from
        L.A.

From the ashes of childhood fires and lost innocence you fashioned a mansion of generosity that I pray will sustain you as long as your aching bones need shelter.

## *Grandpa*

If I had my say
I'd tell them he was
just the kind of grandpa
I would have ordered—
if I'd had a choice.

Who else would have tolerated
a tiny, bespectacled, squeamish
child attempting to bait a
fishhook with red squirmers,
and patiently teach the art
of disentanglement?

Who else would have driven
Old Nell and her buggy
over the church-house hill
to the "stettle" at a clip
unterrifyingly clopped
to placate a small girl nestled
trustingly under his shoulder?

Who else would have allowed
me to feed yellow-orange ears
into the dark hollow that
gushed firm gold nuggets in front
and kicked fuzzy mauve stubs
out the back while squeaky
cogs turned on each other?

Who else would provoke
such clucking with his
shoo-fly pie at breakfast,
black-peppered ice cream,
raw oyster binges at midnight
and pork at any time?

And who, by his absence,
would still evoke melancholy
never consoled by the memory
of one gnarled outstretched palm
slowly pumping good-by
from its stretcher as
the ambulance pulled away
for the last time.

## Sunday Sermons

Apple blossoms in the churchyard
kissing cheeks,
they stood white-capped
in a single row
around the open wood porch
fronting the austere white rectangle, unsteepled,
their plain dresses adorned only with
white organdy capes and aprons
rustling slightly in spring's caress
like virgins prepared to
meet their bridegrooms,
voices hushed as the Sabbath peace

inevitably suspended

when shrill calls
of guinea fowl,
invisible below the hill,
pierced their reverie
like jarring warnings before
the sermon even began
to admonish them the world
was on the threshold with
each step taken outside the flock,
outside the elders' ways,
which some, under their white caps,
thought worthy of exploration
in order to find their peace.

### Light in the Hay Mow

A girl child of eight
is still wide-eyed every time
the haymow delights her

with mewling nests of
cashmere-coated kittens that
erase the loneliness of solitary play

with bluish duck eggs ripe and rotten
to throw through cracks in the mow
on unsuspicious backs of cows

with sudden shafts of light through
narrow windows in hay bale rooms
large enough for laughter, imaginary teas

with tunnels, labyrinths and ladders
inviting exploration

unless

the light on the hay is darkened
by a playmate's connivance to
"teach" her how life begins

the dark sneaks into her gut
like ashes left cold in the stove
with "what ifs" she cannot own

the fear breeds determination,
the strength to say "no more!"
—no play in the hay in the dark

II

A woman goes with the light and the fear
all the way to El Salvador

where desire in human form
calls her name, his shadow
beckoning like a dark star
through the wooden slats
of the night gate

till she moves to answer,
but light awakens;
fear keeps her rooted,
the door secured.

where, caught in torrents
kilometers from home,
she accepts a lift offered by
men and their women
and finds too late
one sot insisting
she read Ecclesiastes
there in the rain,
in the van, among the five
who remember their Creator,
see the light, and set her free.

where she flees honey'd prose flung from village doorways
by that black dog, Don Matias,
no mere young Don Juan,
only to hear one day his steps
like a curse hounding her
on an empty path by Santo Tomas
where with a shield of prayer
and Gospel sword she leaves
the dark one speechless
in the sudden light.

where she discovers
the Light was all along.

## Shadows

Soft lantern shadows
bouncing off white adobe
etched your face god-like
as your voice sang the light
among listeners weary after
the day's long struggle
subduing the earth.

You submerged with song
the anger, the loud accusations
the arguments
that spun endlessly
like the bougainvillea
over the earthen wall
of your mother's bitterness.

A curl of dark hair you left
one day on a kitchen table
interrupted the regular
rhythm of a heart, unlike
the coils and springs
of watches you repaired.

Your sculpted hands
chiseled from rare forest trees
chairs and tables, a small
wooden mold for mud bricks
to complement a lesson in geography
for a teacher who could not map
her own inner continent.

Yet she sensed the call
to the valley of the shadow,
not knowing you would be
summoned the day you swam
with shoes the lake filled,
water reclaiming the body it birthed,
the spirit returning unto Him
who gave it.

*For Fernando

V

*Innocent Abroad*

When I first set foot on foreign soil
I knew less than the six year-olds
entering the wire-fenced aqua-coated
school at the dusty edge of Texistepeque.

They knew

the cashew nut hangs like
a half curled grub attached
below brilliant red fruit enticing
the mouth for a moment before
juicy rapture erupts in itchy pox.

the peach deserves to blush
beside sweet mangos de oro,
de indio, de cuchillo,
de rosa deliciosa
dripping nectar of paradise.

They knew

a toad could grow large enough
to support the weight of a startled
bare foot in a half-moonlit patio
and sicken to death a dog
who dares attack.

a lizard, like some vestige
of a dinosaur running loose
on vines in rugged hills,
could end up bewitching the
partaker of a savory stew.

They knew

the roofs of the town are
predictable as an onset of hiccups,
tiles crashing crazily when the earth
heaves at any moment for days
and nights, cracking adobe walls.


the chief rooster does not wait for morning
to make announcements but heeds an
invisible commander, joined by
the whole village of courtyard criers,
especially when the earth trembles

They knew

the day of the dead draws
pistols, silver blades flashing
onto cobblestone streets
reeking intoxication
after cemetery dues are paid.

the strength of a child to
lead an unsteady man home
to hide shame in the shadow
of his own house, rather than
lie on the sidewalk in front of mine.

They knew I had to learn

how to balance on my head
a brimming kettle from distant *pila*
when water evaporates from the
one faucet outside my kitchen window
like the butterfly over the courtyard wall.

how to fashion from a soggy lump
of ground corn and firm slaps
a perfect antidote for loneliness with
beans and rice Niña Olivia never failed
to set before one lost *gringa*.

I also learned

how many ways my words and actions
could cross a line more definite
than the Tropic of Cancer,
and still be forgiven.

### *"They"*

Like their cousins
standing silently in the presence
of medicine born at earth's dawning,
They held their peace,
brown Latino faces upturned at
identical angle in orderly attention
under the great white tent
hosting foreign guests
eating beans and rice before
starting the day's work.

For morning meditation
They drank eagerly
their prophet's Words of life,
like the bottled water
consumed constantly on site
in searing southern sun,
while do-gooders deaf
to holy silence continued
to spin the air with buzz
that stung the open hands
of their interpreters.

Alone
on the margins,
I saw the shadow of
my father's face
among the brown ones
likewise turned, silent
before God's anointed,
always believing
any language, any place,
worthy of reverence,
any person deserving
an undivided ear.

### *Veracruz, Mexico*

After *café con leche*
we asked here, asked there
found a bus to La Antigua old and wild.
walked sweaty one kilometer
past sugar cane
past shaded tile roofs
past sweet-smelling *yerba buena*,
green tipped cacti shriveled low,
past the *flor de fuego, clavell*
one small muddy white pig
snoozing under spread-armed giant
pointing into shadowed lane
found Cortez not home,
his 1523 dwelling dripping roots
from foliaged sky creeping down
algaed walls of coral brick and stone
smothering life
like midnight in the garden
of mostly evil
obscuring bloody past
en la plaza
salmon-colored *iglesia*'s
blue & white crepe paper
streamers dangled by
prostrate Jesus glass-vaulted
while pigeons ledged overhead
in daylight
pooping on plaster saints
casting sharp angled glances

questioning four hundred years
of goings on below
including *cavallos* Santa Ana
stalled in the convent 1803

and a river ran through it

we tiptoed over swaying bridge
drank *cocobana tortito*
marched back by La Ceiba
where Cortez tied his boat
ate *tamales de elote* so *bueno*
we had *dos cada uno*
sweated one kilometer back
passed sugar cane
inhaling *la fragancia*
back in Nina Chinda's field
back in Santo Tomas 1975
back to *amor en mi corazon*
for this place of gentle *gente*
unhurried
like the river
like the roots,
like the Veracruzanos portside
bouncing babies, dancing lizards,
diving for pesos, dodging bubbles
watching the iron hulled India
roll out humped Volkswagons
from its whalish belly
clouds streaming Carribean pink
lighthouse unlit

U.S. Coast Guard unguarded;
*en el Zocalo* we watched
braided beauty
unfold long skirts like
cream colored swans
swirl and smile their
romeos into the night
into the light
into the night.

## *Babel*

China afternoon in frigid blue Harbin—
unwinding after another morning
wrestling too many English details,
I whip-stepped my usual route by the railroad,
north side of campus on the flat plains,
head tucked into down jacket,
hoping to escape notice by a pack of
dark leather jackets and fur caps bent
intently over a booklet, arguing like crows
around a shiny new cycle, trying to
decipher rules for its inner workings.

Long foreign noses, alas, cannot hide.

Surrounding me, their fingers jabbed at print as
they peered and waited in vain for my explanation.
They flung in my face hands streaked with
Chinese characters in case I was from some
far-flung province sharing their script, not sounds.
They bombarded my ears as if I was deaf.
Finally, I gestured toward the university,
hoping someone there could make
sense of the symbols on the page.

The leader of the pack
ushered me up on the rear of
his newly purchased prestige;
I grasped his waist tentatively
then clung hard as we roared
down an icy alley, slippery as language,
between smoking brick workers' shanties
at campus edge, my prayers escalating
with each twist in the path.

At last, safe near school center,
I spotted Mr. Yu,
my foreign affairs protector
and traverser of tongues.
His eyes crinkled to slits as
I handed him control.
He excused me, and became,
for a blessed moment,
God's salvation from
that tower of Babel.

## *Soulmate II*

What was that quickening,
that phantom spirit reappearing
odd moments, odd years in dreams
still young, dark-haired and gentle
though the blade of time and distance
had long parted our ways?

What was that comradeship,
comfortable as worn shoes,
that drew like magnets our spirits
much too young and old,
far too East and West?

If these soulmates were,
can I mourn their loss?

Since I found you on the bench reserved
for foreigners in that Chinese church, your

face not false or fleeting
    wide as tolerance,
deep eyes blue as truth
    holding wonder at the dawn,
shoulders strong enough for tears
    for carrying the weight of solid things,
a heart forgiving careless word and deed
    generous beyond my pinched purse,
hands that know when to hold and let go,

you have become in time the true
soul I cherish beyond any other mate.

### *For I Was a Stranger*

Old bus galumping down Nanjing night
I didn't know where to get off
to meet friends gathering from north and west
in New Year's foggy shadows.

I didn't know where in the dark to get off
till one dim bulb beckoned me in where
I wasn't expected, where a pot-bellied
coal stove gave off bone-warming heat.

One dim bulb beckoned me in where
a woman invited me out for *la mien*
steaming with angel's breath of savory broth
floating quail eggs and greens.

Next day, this woman invited me out;
she lent me a bike and a red plastic poncho
to keep myself dry in a gray Sunday drizzle
riding among an ocean of bright colors to God's house.

She lent me her bike and red plastic poncho,
asked this lone soul to her birthday feast
of simmering chicken, potatoes, and carrots
in Chinese hot pot with cabbage and leeks.

She asked this lone soul to her birthday feast,
hosting more than an ignorant stranger,
among us I felt the warmth of Another
who calls to me still.

*Interlude*

Like migratory birds, we foreigners returned
every summer, four weeks for four years,
to study language, indoor semantics that left our
brains stressed and strained with tones and characters
that spilled out evenings onto a flat open rooftop.

It was a place to meet between giant hulks in the harbor
and rugged mountains jutting above city pollution
after the daytime heat had walked over the hill.

The rooftop opened space to mark birthdays, any day,
with orb-shaped balloons, anemic pale cakes—
to lose our faces in cool ripe melon, spit seeds with
the day's frustrations over the edge or into the
flowered granite washbasin set on the center post;

to stretch fully on foam mattresses dragged
off beds to soften concrete and catch a falling star,
or sit under moonlight in the strum and song of
our communion.

The rooftop opened space to make peace between
the past year's accumulation of useless gripes
—no heat, red tape, tangled relationships—
and untrod paths of the year ahead.

## Lijiang, China

if we return to the village
by Jade Dragon Snow Mountain
reflected in Black Dragon pool

if the earth swallowed the grandmother
with dark bound feet sleeping
in afternoon light inside her
doorway by the canal

if the foreigner still waits, frying goat cheese
til his native dove finds release
to fly with him away

if Dr. Hu still gathers rare specimens
to cure common and uncommoners
stopping by his gate on a summer day

if he still points to faint tracks in grassy
flats reminding him of Allied pilots
who taught him English

if the young still defy Mao, playing
Naxi lutes and bobos showing off
diversity for national propaganda

if the children still speak
to the elders in the language
of the trees

if the trees still are.

# VI

## Rooted in Earth

*The earth is the Lord's*
*        and all the fullness thereof.* —Psalm 24:1

*Give me strength to walk the soft earth,*
*        a relative to all that is.* —Black Elk

When I was young,

the red earth scrunched feet on rocky hillsides,
became a clay village with roads and houses.

fresh tilled earth swallowed winter feet,
seeds scattered in rows and hills.

farmyard earth in silage rings held stinky feet
grubbing for red worms to catch hungry fish.

moist earth oozed between toes by the springhouse,
crayfish and salamanders sheltered in shadows.

spongy earth on creek banks held firmly planted feet,
fingers plucked fresh green mint for summer tea.

springy earth of emerald beckoned
bronzed bare feet into the open pasture.

Later,

hollowed earth held rooted feet on the early autumn day
the Arkansas River infused me with its rushing,
a school of rainbow trout barely noting posts of flesh as
they streamed through and around like extended dashes.

packed earth guided dusty feet to Nina Chinda's hut
with an earthen floor that held me close one day
gunshot exploded silence across the cornfield
between the hills by Monte del Padre.

terraced earth on Sichuan mountains cradled
muddy feet, bent backs, wide brimmed hats,
beds for cabbage, broccoli, spinach, rice
and a road winding the foreigner round and round

frozen earth held bundled feet exploring Harbin's
frozen ice-castles, pagodas, the park by Songhua Jiang
holding crystal figurines of dancing ballarinas, butting
buffalo, Cinderella coaches, lucky fish, lighted slides

I learned,

soft earth is what sore feet long for

green earth is what eyes drink after a drought

digging earth ejects the rubbish soiling inner thought.

a space on earth is what is left when wind and fire consume
    what was there.

giving earth transforms, with rain, the seed, the sapling, to multiply its treasures.

Tread gently on earth.

## Clean Air Act

What do they know
—the crows circling in waving clouds
above the hemlocks bordering our
usually serene morning wake-up walks?

The sky fills with raucous irreverent news
growing shriller as one more comes
from the north, a pair flies from the south,
another from the west
to swell the black caucus
now swirling, now alighting
covering a few staunch bare maples on
the highest points of the hill
like mourner's bows stuck to each branch.

Have they seen
the veiled winks, the surreptitious nudges,
the lifting of cowardly hands,
the cowardly stroke of the pen
of a mostly white caucus
blind to rolling emerald pastures, wooded
shades of green I cannot name
sheltering brilliant song and feather,
blind to spongy velvet carpets
fit for a forest queen,
blind to living dancing green touched with breath of
the Divine, now on the brink,
blind to all but the color green
      stamped with the face of a man?

## *Holy Ire*

The day we youth,
set free from walls and chairs,
explored canyon bluffs
wrapped in winter's fleece,
edges of rocks hung
with gleaming ice
clear as crystal,
extended grace
ravishing
the fairy kingdom

my anger
pulsed clean and pure
bone deep
when from some
dark heart
a giant stone was hurled,
smashing in an instant
splendid cones
formed in hours
in days
drip by drip.

I still burn
to see one shining
jewel shattered,
one sovereign sight
in haste erased by
those mindless of
the Heart that grieves
to see one sparrow fall.

**Water**

bursts like a giant balloon,
drops and splatters in every
direction inescapably bent
on dousing everything
under heaven, rivers
course downhill through
the yard forming
a pool by the mailbox
where neighborhood
children sail paper boats,
then creeps down the cellar
stairs poking long wet fingers
under the basement door.

Water and wind toppled
mighty trunks across
the path we walked today
leaving birds speechless
wind passed on
but water speaking still
in merry little trickles
dropping from gigantic
dark roots exposed
like a Hobbit's den
on the hill above,
sunlight captured in
each liquid jewel
varnishing mossy banks
while chipmunks

hightail sleek stripes
and scold intruders for
interrupting crickets'
water symphonies.

Our feet trudge on, leaving
prints in soggy path
skirting muddied pools
towards the indomitable
rushing clarified
in one crystal plunging
stream before us
like Pure Grace.
We sit on a stone wall
observing on the cliff
a lone sapling
hosting a community
of walking sticks that
mate unashamed
without love or violence,
matter-of-factly,
while a blue-striped
purple-tailed lizard
soaks up the wall's
warmth before
rain comes again.

## Snake Stories

The rattlesnake
sprawled on the warm boulder beside
blueberry bushes I was stripping
one young summer day,
did not bother to inform me he was there
or give me a dose of his lethal injection.

Nor did a copperhead
calmly weaving its way
in the dusk from one side
of the stony mountain trail to the other
pause to strike needlessly at my feet,
an inch from fangs that could have
given me fever and hallucination.

Neither did the fer-de-lance,
gliding like a mottled meter-long rope
over my petrified feet in the patio,
threaten me with a fatal dose of venom
as he disappeared into the dim recess
of my open kitchen.

Not even did the coral snake
curled under long cool tropical grasses
bent over the path I trod with sandaled feet,
seem interested in needless exertion and
human paralysis on a steamy afternoon.

Now I tremble when the Bushsnake
sends more unsuspecting tender species
into situations seething with
poisons of soul, feverish hallucinations
and paralyses worse than
the lethal strikes,
the fatal venom
of all other snakes.

### Temples

Silently they file into dimness,
candles sparse, shorn heads inclined,
white robes flowing
like the Holy Ghost hovering
over morning Laud, crossing arms
bowing to the cross, bearing their cross
singing one thousand year old hymns
to God the Father in solemn harmony
while a choir strikes vibrant chords
outside the sunlit door:

song sparrow
      redwing
brown thrasher
      robin
mockingbird
      bluebird
meadowlark
      goldfinch
purple finch
      titmouse
towhee
a cardinal
without a robe
    without a cross
        without walls

laud within their temple.

## *Tom's Garden*

Blueberries, raspberries, dewberries, plums
Apple trees border this whimsical patch.

Peonies, poppies, potatoes, petunias
Ivy creeps sideways up a stone wall.

Burdocks, onions, and coral bells
Grapevines tangle with sumac and beech.

Clover and comfrey, cosmos and catnip
Boxwoods protect a pedestaled dial.

Teasel, tomatoes, tarragon, thyme
Lilies are clothed without spinning at all.

Violets and rhubarb, lilac and zinnia
Morning glories vine from earth to sky.

Moonflowers, goldenrod, daisies and roses
Forsythias bow at the ancestor's gate.

Through these and all within my glance
May the wind weave forever in holy dance.

## Life Cycles

I.
The long winter left leaves dry
as old skin littering the lawn, bare
knobby limbs like aged legs, spent
deadheads of last year's dill and sunflowers.

Yet, as I clipped bleached dry fronds
on tall grasses bordering the garden
pale green shone from the core,
waiting between winter and summer
to emerge new and brave.

II.

Her skin was dry and wrinkled as
old potatoes, limbs bent and brittle as
the stems of last year's peonies, hair faded
like dead twigs piled in the corner of the yard.

Yet, as I dressed her frailty in fresh clothes,
her eyes, still vibrant, sparkled as
she joked about preparing for a date,
the next moment asking for her long passed husband,
her spirit suspended between youth and age.

## *The Author*

Esther Stenson, Harrisonburg, Virginia, spent her childhood and teenage years in a progressive Amish community in Stuarts Draft, Virginia. At the time, this community sanctioned public school education through seventh grade and provided parochial education from grades eight to ten.

At age twenty-one, Stenson taught in a local church school. Later, she spent nearly three years teaching in El Salvador (1974-77) under Amish Mennonite Missions and finally attended Sterling College in Kansas (1980-84).

After graduation, she taught English in Harbin, China, for a year before returning to the U.S. for TESOL graduate studies at Georgetown University. She spent four more years teaching English in China, after which she and her husband (whom she met in China) returned to Harrisonburg, Virginia (1995).

Since then, she has been employed at James Madison University in Harrisonburg, curently teaching Freshman Composition and British Literature. She also completed a Master's Degree in English Literature and Creative Writing at JMU in 2008. She and her husband attend Community Mennonite Church.

www.ingramcontent.com/pod-product-compliance
Lightning Source LLC
Chambersburg PA
CBHW030001050426
42451CB00006B/76